Y0-AVB-118

JINGLES
for the
JANG LED

Mary Paxton "Pax" Kirby

Not a book for deep-poetry lovers.
You'll find some jingles between its covers
Just a rhythmic way of trying my best
to get one or two things off my chest.

And, please remember, it's mostly in jest.

TABBY HOUSE BOOKS

Paperback Trade Inn
145 East Fourteen Mile Rd
Clawson, MI 48017
(248) 307-0226

Copyright © 1992 Mary Paxton Kirby

All rights reserved; no part of this publication may be reproduced, stored in a retrieval system, or transmitted, in any form or by any means, electronic, mechanical, photocopying, recording, or otherwise, without the prior written permission of Mary Paxton Kirby.

Manufactured in the United States of America.

Library of Congress Number: 92-085240
Second Printing, April 1993

ISBN: 1-881539-00-8

TABBY HOUSE BOOKS

4429 Shady Lane, Charlotte Harbor, FL 33980
813-629-7646, FAX 813-629-4270

Disclaimer

The views and opinions
expressed in the following
pages do not necessarily
coincide with those of my
husband, Durward Kirby,
to whom, I nevertheless
dedicate this book.

Who Said, "Nothing Rhymes With Orange"?

As I behold the purple finch
I know one thing that is a cinch.
As he flutters up within our range
He's mostly brown and sometimes orange.
Believe me, let it here be said,
He is not purple, he is red.
Whoever named him, in my mind,
Surely must have been color-blind.

Contents

Dedication	*iii*
Who Said, "Nothing Rhymes With Orange"?	*iii*
Preface	*vi*
My Good Old Smith-Corona	7
Men in the Kitchen	9
Stay Out of My Kitchen	10
Christmas Shopping	12
It's the Thought that Counts	13
Shopping in the Mall	14
A Jaundiced Look at the Movies	15
Peace: Wouldn't it be Wonderful?	17
The Dinner Party	18
The Wrap-Around Skirt	20
Emphasis on Being Thin	21
The Mirror	22
They Say a Mirror Never Lies	23
What's for Dinner?	24
What Can We Eat?	25
Jaded Palate? No!	27
The Size of Eggs	28
The Age of Invention	30
Fractured by Fractions	32
My Secret Failing	34
Ear Pollution	35
Shrieks a la Mode	36
Have I Missed the Boat Somewhere?	38
Why Do I have to Do It?	39
The Thankless Task	41
Transportation	42
Flying	44
On the Menu There was Fish	46
Letting the Mind Hang Loose	47
Some Thoughts on Gravity	48
What Ever Happened to the Moth?	50
Facing Up	51

The Importance of a Will............................53
Children..54
A Look at Having Children.......................56
Dear Son..58
Response..60
The VCR and Other TV Devices...................61
Sneaky TV.......................................63
Beards..64
Men Who Wear Beards.............................65
The State Lottery...............................66
Reading About the Rich and Famous..............67
The National Enquirer...........................68
Holidays..69
Holidays (Like Mother's and Father's)..........70
What's His Name.................................72
A Special Tribute...............................74

To Nolia, With Love.............................74

Poems of Inspiration–From the Heart

Remembering.....................................76
God's Gift, the Sunrise.........................77
My Dawn Comes Softly............................78
I looked to the Hills...........................79
Soft Music......................................79
With Love to Tyler..............................80
Love Before First Sight.........................81
God Bless This Child............................82
Patience..83
You Can Do It!..................................83
She Loves Me....................................84
The Invisible Tie...............................85
Friendship......................................85
Love is Forever.................................86
The Chickadee...................................87

About the Author

Preface

It is not the big problems in our lives that rattle our brains and fill us with stress. It is the little things that we dwell on, and can't seem to do anything about, that build up nervous tension.

In this book of prose and verse, I have attempted to bring some of these nerve jangling things into the light so they can be examined for what they are worth. My hope is that, by poking fun at them, we will be able to reduce them to their proper place of unimportance.

Being able to laugh at ourselves and the antics of the world around us, is, to my mind, the quickest way back to the center of the road.

~

Please join me first on my trip through the instruction book of this brand-new, yet untried, electronic typewriter.

My Good Old Smith-Corona

My old Smith-Corona
Went into a coma.
It would not type
And I had to write.

Since its illness was described as chronic
I chose to try a new electronic.
Now I find I am in a daze
Facing this new computered maze.

It's filled with buttons quite mysterious.
To me, it's a problem very serious.
It has lights and little print-out screens.
I'll never learn what each one means.

I timidly touched the key "indent,"
And off the roller my typing went.
The shift key didn't seem to engage.
The carrier flew right off the page.

Another key I touched down lower
Sent pages flying to the floor!
This devilish thing's too much for me.
I'm losing my identity.

It has a memory better than mine.
All well and good, that's very fine.
But when I want it to recall
I can not make it work at all.

Now here is a button I have never used.
What does it mean? I'm so confused.
What it will do, only heaven knows.
Oh my! I touched it and there it Gooooooes#&(s!!!!!

I must be a throw-back to some other age.
It takes me forever to write just one page.
On this new, intimidating contraption,
I can't seem to make the required adaption.

I think that I'd be very wise,
To take an ad and advertise.
Will somebody, please, who is an owner
Sell me his good old Smith-Corona?

Men in the Kitchen

Some men are born cooks. Their lucky wives have never had to cook a meal since the day they first set up housekeeping. The men come home from the office and head for the kitchen simply because they love to cook.

Granted, these men are a rarity, and there is another side of the coin. There is the man who has retired, and up until now has never set foot in the kitchen in his whole life, except to mix a drink.

Around the house a lot now, with nothing much to do, he decides to become a gourmet cook, starting with a book on French cuisine. Or he buys a wok and goes gung-ho over Chinese.

The result of his afternoon spent destroying the kitchen is a concoction that is edible only if you are a raccoon. The reason is that he got carried away and added touches of his own to the recipe. He has not yet learned that oregano does not go into everything.

When he finally tires of this occupation, he begins supervising his wife's cooking. He will tell her how to make something she has been cooking all her married life.

My husband appointed himself pot-watcher one evening when I was cooking dinner for guests. It was a chicken casserole that took a couple of hours to bake, and gave me plenty of time to visit with my guests before dinner.

Later that evening, after I had served the dish and we were seated at the table, I tried to cut into the chicken on my plate. To my horror, I discovered the chicken was almost raw.

It turned out that my spouse had wandered into the kitchen while I was getting dressed. He peeked into the glass window of the oven and saw the casserole was bubbling. Meaning to be helpful, and without a word to me, he lowered the heat.

What do you do in a case like that? Take everyone out to McDonald's?

Husbands are not the only ones who can ruin a dinner. Take guests, for instance....

Stay Out of My Kitchen

When I am trying to prepare a meal,
I know it isn't a very big deal.
But I'd rather be alone in the kitchen
When a dinner for guests, I'm out there fixin'.

Certain guests seem to think that they will be
Awarded a medal for helping me.
They always have a lot to say,
But only manage to get in my way.

Their chatter breaks my concentration,
It causes me much aggravation.
They stand where the drawer that is essential
Is holding my most needed utensil.

When I want to wash my hands,
By the sink my good friend stands.
Leaning and talking with drink in hand,
Who will only move on my demand.

It's impossible to turn out haute cuisine,
When a wandering guest is on the scene.
I'm distracted, befuddled, I forget my holder.
I burn my thumb, she's standing right by my
    shoulder.

I rush to the fridge to put a thumb on ice.
By now, I find I have scorched the wild rice!
The dinner is well on its way to disaster.
Alone, I could have cooked it better and faster.

I've often longed to put up a sign:
Go away! Stay out! This kitchen is mine!
I don't need help, any one to pitch in.
No one is welcome in a one-butt kitchen.

Christmas Shopping

Every year, along about August, something pushes the fast forward button in my mind and hastens my thoughts ahead to December and my resolution to do my Christmas shopping early.

I fantasized about how great it would be to just sit back during the pre-holiday rush, watching my less organized friends tearing around wearing themselves out in crowds of last minute shoppers.

With this delightful image to cheer me on, I went to my favorite department store. My visions of tinsel, red ribbons and sleigh bells vanished when I entered the store. I saw nothing but racks and counters filled with things of summer—on sale for the thrifty to buy now for next year.

Since stores keep advertising Christmas earlier and earlier, perhaps I was tricked into thinking that they might have started in August. I resisted thrift and I didn't take advantage of the sales. If I can't project my thoughts ahead four months to Christmas, how in heaven's name could I possibly know what I will want next summer?

If I run true to form, I will think of what I need for summer about the end of May when the stores start showing fall woolens and fur coats. As I looked around the store, I noticed that they did have the Halloween decorations up. But really, you can't give someone a pumpkin for Christmas! Hmmmmm...or can you? Without doubt, I will join the throng of last minute shoppers after Thanksgiving. When the last hastily-bought present is wrapped and sent, I will pray to God that I didn't forget anyone and fervently hope that I don't have to stand in line at the exchange desk after the holiday.

It's the Thought That Counts

There are things we often forget to do.
We mean well, but we neglect them, too.
There are many times when we have failed
To get that special birthday card mailed
On time for a friend, who's loved, to get it
On the proper day—and we regret it.

There are holidays when we procrastinate.
Let Christmas shopping go 'til nearly too late.
We nervously scan all the names on our list.
Buying "just anything" is hard to resist,
To get the whole business out of the way;
So something will be there on Christmas day.

We justify this thought as stress and strain mounts,
By telling ourselves it's "just the thought that counts."
It's comforting to know we're not alone in this.
Other people, too, are likely to be remiss.
Think back to the times your man opened a box
And found something, like a pair of bright pink socks.

It bends your mind, you stand wondering why,
Anyone would send *pink* to a macho guy.

Mary Paxton Kirby

Shopping in the Mall

Christmas once was a time of snow,
To bundle up as cold winds blow.
Christmas shopping
Kept us hopping,
From store to store in cold wet sleet,
As we went slogging down each street.
While church bells chimed in sweet euphonia,
We took a chance on getting pneumonia.
Then someone came along and invented The Mall,
So the weather became no problem at all.

Now we shop in almost summer-like ease,
With no more fear of that dreaded disease.
Electronically, carols now are pealed,
As we listen to them, hermetically sealed.
It all seems so nice
But we pay the price.
We are shopping in a very crowded condition.
Pneumonia might seek us by transmission.

On top of that, in this fresh air-less box,
We might even catch the chicken pox!
I take just a moment to digress.
Let me ask you, *This*...is progress?

A Jaundiced Look at the Movies

I don't go to the movies much any more. When I find a movie with a cast and subject that appeals to me, nine times out of ten, the producers will spoil it by inserting a shocking episode that the production would have been much better off without.

I have read that this is a ploy to get the picture an R or X rating. They say that without these ratings, no one would come to the theater. Have we come to the point where we no longer value good taste?

For instance: Take a look at the charming story, *E.T.* Because there was no sex or nudity to titillate the erotic tastes of certain movie-goers, what did they do? They had the writers put four letter words into the mouths of the otherwise engaging little children in the story. Deplorable.

It added nothing to the story and was in exceedingly bad taste. I wanted to take hold of the producers and writers and wash *their* mouths out with soap.

Another reason I don't go to the movies often is because many of them are filled with violence. We don't have to go to the movies for that. We get enough of it on the six o'clock news.

When I take the trouble to get dressed up, hop in the car, take the risk of being mugged in the parking lot, and pay today's inflated prices for admission...I want to see something that makes me think, or lets me leave the theater, in a happy frame of mind, knowing that I had a good time.

I miss the romance of the old movies and their good taste. To my notion, *It Happened One Night,* with Claudette Colbert and Clark Gable was a far more sexy movie than any of the bare-bottomed movies of today.

The director left the sex to the viewer's imagination. At the end of the picture, when the blanket that was hung between the beds finally came down...WOW!

Today it's boy meets girl. Then without any pretense of courting or getting to know each other, almost before the cast credits stop rolling on the screen, they are nude and going at it in bed. YUK!

So many bare bodies are becoming ho-hum. To me, a sweaty nude body will never be as sexy or as exciting as a Cary Grant, impeccably dressed in a white tie and tails.

Instant sex scenes, without a shred of romance preceding them, bore the hell out of me.

Peace: Wouldn't it be Wonderful?

How do we ever hope to attain world peace if we can't get along with each other in our own little circle of friends and neighbors?

The least little disagreement between two friends can sometimes result in a major blowup.

A thoughtless remark, a slip of the tongue or a statement repeated out of context by a gossipy person can spread animosity all out of proportion to the trivial remark that started it.

In a case like this, sides start to be drawn and that leads to the disintegration of what was once a happy circle of pals.

When are we going to stop listening to second-hand gossip and go directly to the source of our hurt feelings to straighten things out?

So many hurts can be healed by getting the facts or opening a chance for the offender to say a sincere..."I'm so sorry."

Good friends are hard to come by. People we really love and enjoy being with are to be treasured. We can miss a lot of fun by getting our feathers ruffled by what are really small things.

For example: Look at what happened to my husband and me when we wanted to celebrate an important anniversary last year.

Mary Paxton Kirby

The Dinner Party

One time I decided to have a party.
A sit down dinner, not formal or arty.
I wanted to ask only six or eight
Of my very best friends right up to date.

I ran into problems....here is the gist.
It started when I made out my list.
Mary Jones and Peggy Schiff,
Recently had had a tiff.

George Brown and his buddy, Hamilton
    Rolfe,
Were out of sorts over a game of golf.
I remembered–Lilly Smith and Margaret
    O'Day
Weren't speaking. Something happened at
    the P.T.A.

Jim Johnson and dear old Harry O'Neill,
Had fallen out over a business deal.
In view of all this, I simply was not
    able,
To seat all of these people at the same
    table.

It really turned out to be quite a task.
These were the friends I wanted to ask.
I started to call but hung up the phone.
My husband and I had dinner alone.

THE DINNER PARTY

Mary Paxton Kirby

The Wrap-Around Skirt

Years ago, fashion came up with a design,
That is a perennial favorite of mine.
Easy to don and quick to get out of,
One of the reasons I'm so very fond of,
The wrap-around skirt that's so easy to wear.
It will go to the grocery, a party or fair.
Today you can buy them appliqued,
Hand-painted too, it has been said.
But nothing is perfect in this old world.
They have a tendency to come unfurled,
When you walk down the street and the wind is
    blowing,
You must grab with both hands if your skirt starts
    flowing.
Because if you don't, when the wind gets quite high,
It'll unveil your panties to the passers-by!

Emphasis on Being Thin

There is so much emphasis on being thin.
The ads all picture everyone slim.
I get a feeling of inferiority,
I suspect too, that a great majority,
Feel the same way when they look into mirrors
And see what's bulging on their posteriors.

I feel guilt go surging into my head,
Whenever I eat a piece of bread.
Heaven forbid, that I should take,
Even a look at a chocolate cake!
Why is it always considered a sin,
If we're not emaciatedly thin?

Some figures just get out of sync,
Because of some metabolic kink.
I could starve myself to anorexia,
Until I was skeletal and I betchia,
Remaining, there would be that
    crummy,
Little, poked out, bulging tummy.

The Mirror

Mirror, mirror, on the wall,
I don't believe your image at all.
I think you are into falsifying.
Either that, or just plain lying.
Who is this person you have put in my place,
Whenever I greet you face to face?
Instead of someone who is young and tall,
There is a stranger there, I don't know at all.
This one has wrinkles *and graying hair.*
You have stolen my youth and it's most unfair!

They Say a Mirror Never Lies
(But sometimes it can deceive)

Your mirror says you are looking so well.
You feel your age is not starting to tell.

Your eyes are sparkling, your step is light.
Your spirit lifts, everything is bright.

Until...some clerk in a store...rings up your bill
And asks you a question that gives you a chill.

The young twerp brings you down and puts you out
    for the count,
By asking, "You want the senior citizen discount?"

23

What's for Dinner?

Being an impressionable sort of person, I have to be very careful about who and what I listen to. The same goes for what I read.

I don't dare look into any kind of medical book because my imagination borders on hypochondria. Tell me the symptoms of some ailment and I transfer them to my body immediately.

It is quite a trick today to tune out this sort of thing. It comes from everywhere.

I go on a diet and think I have conquered my sweet tooth with saccharin and the doctors and experts warn that it could give you......I don't dare say or think the word.

I try to straighten out my nutrition and when I read or listen to advice on the subject, I find that damn near anything I like is on the taboo list.

About the only thing left for me is fiber, and to get enough, I have to buy it in a carton and mix it with water. YUK!

Let's look at the following list and you tell me....What can we eat?

What Can We Eat?

If we pay attention to the FDA,
There's hardly anything we can eat today!
Let's see now...where do we start?
Can't drink coffee...bad for the heart.

Mustn't eat eggs or white bread toast;
Two of the foods we like the most.
Eggs are supposed to give us cholesterol.
For that same reason, we can't butter a roll.

They labeled fat a deadly sin,
They took away our saccharin.
Fresh fruits and vegetables are taboo,
They're sprayed with something that's not good for
    you.

That leaves meat–and perhaps some chicken.
But no, they're filled with penicillin,
Or perhaps some other exotic,
Medicine or antibiotic.

You might think that it sure would be dandy,
To bring your sweetheart a box of candy.
But sugar's another treat not allowed,
Never even mention that word out loud.

Mary Paxton Kirby

It occurred to me that maybe fish,
Might turn out to be our only dish.
Even that was no solution,
Due to pond and sea pollution.

If it's impossible to eat all this,
Think of all the things we are going to miss,
Protecting ourselves from all of these ills,
Dining on fiber and vitamin pills.

Jaded Palate? No!

Looking back over the years, it seems to me that a lot of the foods we ate as children tasted much better then, than they do today.

Now don't tell me that it is a jaded palate that leads me into this belief. I have heard that before. I am going to offer proof.

Let's just examine ice cream as an example. Some companies advertise "ice cream parlor flavor" and others, "all natural ice cream." When I was a child and given a helping of ice cream, like any child, I savored every bite and wanted to make it last as long as possible.

When I ate it down to the last few spoonsful, I would stir it around until it had turned into "soup."

If my mother was looking the other way, I would pick up my bowl with both hands, tip it up to my mouth and drink the cold, creamy delight down to the last delicious drop. There would not even be a scraping left in the bottom of the dish. Try that today!

There have been times when I have just served myself a bowl of ice cream and been called away to the telephone. Fifteen minutes later when I returned, the ice cream was still standing tall in my dish—not melted at all. But it was no longer ice cream. It had turned into a helping of warm, not very tasty pudding.

We have gotten so far away from the original that you can hardly find a recipe with the old ingredients in it.

Additives and preservatives are the probable cause. Whatever, it is fairly easy to see how changes like this could come about, but it is incomprehensible to me how they have been able to change the taste and size of eggs.

I keep looking for a farmer who raises chickens in his back yard, throws some feed on the ground and lets the chickens scratch for it. It would be wonderful to taste a fresh egg, warm from the henhouse again.

The Size of the Eggs

Hey, Mister Nader!
Where is your raider?
Hasn't he detected
That eggs are affected,
By a new kind of grading
That the grocers are trading?

The cartons are marked Jumbo,
Extra-large, Large and Small.
If you look into the matter
They are not that way at all.
They have always been marked
By these same devices
But the difference in size
Today is the prices.

Remember the times you'd
Visit your folks?
They would serve you eggs
With double yolks.
What's going on
In the henhouse nowadays,
That is dwarfing the eggs
In so many ways?

I don't mean to be
Any kind of presumer.
I'm writing to you
Only as a consumer.
A little ol' pigeon standing
On just one leg,
Could lay down one bigger
Than the grocer's hen's egg.

Go after them, Ralph!
Make them label them all small.
There's no difference, we can see
In those eggs at all!

EGGS

The Age of Invention

We live in an age of miraculous invention.
Making life easier is the only intention,
Of many bright men and women, too,
Who want to make life easier for you —
And me — to have more time for pleasure,
To just hang loose and take our leisure.

They gave us the jet to get there quicker,
Lottery numbers with a mechanical picker.
The microwave, the fast food store.
The catalogues and what is more,
No-iron sheets and pillow cases,
Tummy tucks and lifted faces.
Frozen dinners and what do you know?
Hair cuts and curls that are wash and go.

Then came along the home computer,
Smaller each year and so much cuter.
You don't have to learn to add and subtract.
A calculator takes care of that.
They changed the holidays so we could eke
Out living in just a four-day-week.
But there's one thing, it's really a crime,
The little things seem to take much more time.

Why on earth is there such a big gap
In time to remove a medicine cap.
Another thing that makes me scowl
Is trying to unwrap the paper towel!

Or wrestling with that pesky caper
Of changing a roll of toilet paper.
"It's impossible, still," someone has said,
"For a stiff-jointed robot to make a bed."

A dishwasher will make your china so clean,
But tell me, science, what does that mean?
If inventors in this great world today,
Can't teach them to get up and put them away!

Fractured by Fractions

My mother had a firm conviction that one should never let school interfere with a child's education. I was the envy of many of my classmates because of my frequent absences from school.

Whenever my mother wanted to pack up and go somewhere, she used the theory that travel was broadening, as her excuse to yank me out of school and take me along.

In addition to believing that the trips were educational, she was convinced that traveling was healthier for me than sitting in a stuffy, overheated school room, filling my head with dreary facts and breathing chalk into my lungs.

I was like the well-known credit card. Mother never left home without me.

Naturally, like any kid, I loved those trips and particularly because it meant a release from school. My mother and I both thought that "school" was just another word for "jail."

The only problem was that the piper had to be paid when I got home. Even though my school books accompanied me when I went away, I had to run like a bandit to catch up with the rest of the class.

It so happened that while I was basking in the Mississippi sunshine, my classmates up north were busy taking up something called fractions.

My Mother monitored my lessons on the road, but fractions had never been her long suit. Between her inability to teach the subject and my total mystification, we had a problem that neither of us could solve.

That particular trip left a gap in my education from which I have never completely recovered.

Mary Paxton Kirby

My Secret Failing

I'll tell you a secret failing of mine.
I'm going to lay it right on the line.
It's that I'm completely without any talents
When it comes to making my checkbook balance.
It's not that I can't add two plus two
And count the same as most others do.
But there is something about the rigors
Of decoding all those print-out figures
That the bank sends out that keep me busy
With uneven numbers that make me dizzy.
I can't find out the reason why...
Something is wrong whenever I
Add up the totals in my bank's account.
They are not the same as my book's amount.
I go over and over the sums and much later,
Find I can even be wrong with a calculator.

My husband never has any problem with his.
When it comes to math, he's a veritable whiz.
I used to ask him for some help with mine.
For a short time that worked out very fine.
But to him it seems hilariously funny,
That his wife can never keep track of her money.
It has reached a point and to my consternation,
Became the topic of cocktail conversation.
To keep our marriage on an even keel,
I don't let him know how I really feel.
I don't like being an object of fun.
Inside me I know something must be done.
Right here and now I have made up my mind,
Somehow or other I will try to find
A solution to my problem someday, some way.
Does anyone know a good close-mouthed C.P.A.?

Ear Pollution

As though there is not enough noise in the world already, a new bit of ear pollution has been added. This time it has been unleashed by a most unlikely source—babies!

Of course, babies have always cried and even bawled, but now they have learned to shriek! It is amazing to me that a sound that can outstretch Barbra Streisand's highest note can emerge from those tiny little throats and rosebud mouths.

You hear them everywhere, on the street, in stores, churches, and I suppose, even in subways. I wouldn't know about the latter. I gave up riding subways long before the graffiti and muggings started.

Any baby whose mother takes him on the subway has a right to shriek. But to me, that is the only place it might be allowed in public.

The worst thing about this growing trend among the tots is that the parents make no effort to stop it.

I have had my sinuses cleared when a little banshee lets go behind my back in a store and scares my new perm straight again. I draw the line when it happens in a restaurant.

Has the following happened to you? Betcha it has!

Mary Paxton Kirby

Shrieks a La Mode

When we go out to dinner or even for lunch,
No sooner are we seated than in comes a bunch
Of people with children who sit down right next to
    me.
The children are babies, their ages one, two and
    three.
The minute they are high-chaired, one child splits
    the air
With a blood curdling scream that will raise your
    hair.

We look up to see if the child is in pain.
Nothing's wrong as far as we can ascertain.
Our ears are still ringing
From that sound but when you
Look at the parents
They're studying the menu.

The child screams again. Why? Just for the hell of
    it!
The parents act as if quite unaware of it.
Perhaps they are deaf from the loud music they
    love,
That has deadened their ears...but heavens above!
Is it possible that they can't hear a thing?
Not even the shrieks from their tiny offspring?

I put forth my suspicion and I believe it's a fact.
It's a lack of discipline and parents failure to act.

LITTLE SCREAMERS

Have I Missed the Boat Somewhere?

As I have said earlier in this book, I don't watch a whole lot of television any more. However, I have friends who are hooked on the afternoon soaps and wouldn't miss "Donahue" for anything.

They tell me that watching those shows is a learning experience and a sexual education as well.

Where else, they say, could they have ever seen Boy George or male strippers?

I will admit that once in a while I used to take a look at "Dallas" and "Dynasty." When I saw all those glamorous ladies, dressed to the teeth and living in luxurious surroundings without ever having to turn a hand around the house...it gave me pause.

I stop to examine my own lot, and it set me to wondering....

Why Do I Have To Do It?

Eleanor Roosevelt never did it.
If she did, she certainly hid it.
Nancy Reagan doesn't have to do it.
Elizabeth Taylor would eschew it.
Barbra Streisand would say to shove it.
The Queen of England's way above it.
The sisters Gabor would not pursue it.
Not on your life did they ever do it!

(I'm sure most men would never do it.
Although they think there is nothing to it.)

Is there some kind of unfair injunction
That Fate has laid down for *me* to function
Otherwise from all those listed above?
Why was I chosen for a life whereof
My days are not mine to command.
I truly do not understand.
I do the same things every day,
Monday, Tuesday, right through Sunday.

It's do the dishes, make the beds,
Dust the halls and clean the heads.
Wash the laundry, there is always a ton of it!
Nobody does that just for the fun of it!
I call on the powers above and below.
Won't you tell me? I would really like to know
The answer to the question that is to wit,
Why me? Just why was *I* chosen to do it?

The Thankless Task

Each morning as I make up a bed
Other things I'd rather do instead.
It's the impermanence of it that gets to me...
A thankless task to be done over endlessly!

After you have struggled to make one up,
A few hours later, it's all torn up.
When doing housework, you know how it goes.
It's more satisfying when your work shows.

I'd really prefer to have the employment,
Of baking a pie for family enjoyment.
It's gone in a few minutes but after they ate it
They told me how much it was appreciated.

Compliments come and it's not quite such a trial.
It's nice to be told you've done something worth-
    while.
To what housewife has it ever been said?
"Dear, you *sure* know how to *make up a bed!*"

41

Transportation

One of my big problems today is transportation. The airlines have robbed me of one of my greatest pleasures. They have almost put the railroads out of business.

Because of my long-time love affair with passenger trains, I can selfishly wish that Orville and Wilbur had never gotten off the ground at Kittyhawk.

I was hooked on trains forever, in childhood, when my mother first took me overnight on a Pullman. I was captivated watching the efficiency with which the porter pulled out the seats and backs of the facing green plush seats and turned them into a bed.

When the upper berth was pulled down from the ceiling, it enclosed my section into a snug little room that was all my own.

I loved to lie tucked in with my doll and my shoes bedded down in the small green mesh hammock that was slung on hooks across the double windows of my berth.

Unable to sleep from excitement, I would prop myself up on pillows and squeeze the brass latch that operated the dark green window blind.

I would open it just enough so that with the lights turned out, no one could see me in the darkness, but I could watch the small towns fly by as the train blasted its whistle and the warning bells at the crossing sang their merry tune.

After a while, my eyes would grow heavy while the clickety-clack of the wheels and the motion of the train gently lulled me to sleep.

No sleeping pill ever invented could top that.

It is hard for me to believe that most young people have never ridden overnight on a passenger train.

There is a small resurgence of interest in railroads now because they are considered an oddity. Old, comfortable day coaches are being refurbished to take people for short trips through scenic countryside. They are much like a ride at Disneyland.

However, that sort to thing will never give anyone a clear picture of the thrill and luxury of riding, sleeping and dining on trains such as the 20th Century Limited and the Super Chief.

Airplanes, admittedly, get you there in a hurry, but you never see the beautiful, changing countryside that stretches from coast to coast in America. And luxurious? They are **not.**

The old, uncomfortable day coach has returned. Only this time, it's thirty thousand feet up in the air.

Flying

I don't like to fly in aeroplanes.
I much prefer a luxury train.
I really have no fear of flying.
Some of my friends believe I'm lying.

I'll admit I have some trepidation
About flying off to a foreign nation.
You board a plane for London or Japan,
And wind up as a hostage in Iran!

I know that the odds are very small.
I don't give much thought to that at all.
It's the little things that don't appeal to me,
'Cause I have a small peculiarity.

I have never liked to travel en masse,
But it's expensive to travel first class.
When sealed in a plane I get a phobia:
Acro, claustro, and xeno phobia.

I'm uncomfortable sitting next to strangers.
I keep contemplating all the awful dangers
Of being seated next to someone's child
Who's eating chocolate and acting wild.

Who puts smeary fingers on my lap.
Who could surely use a well-placed slap.
Or...of being placed in a seat beside
A talkative bore for the whole damn ride.

A plane, to me, is like an aluminum tin,
Hermetically sealed and filled to the brim.
I'll tell you exactly what I mean.
It makes me feel just like a sardine!

When Edison saw a plane take so long to get off,
He considered it thoughtfully...but he didn't scoff.
He saw difficulties ahead, too many to mention.
But he simply said, "It's not a finished invention."

Right on, Mr. Edison! It's plain to see,
If you were still here, you'd agree with me.

Mary Paxton Kirby

On the Menu There was Fish

I was feeling very bright and perky,
As the train pulled into Albuquerque.
The porter told me he was going out
To pick up an order of mountain trout.

That night on the menu, there was the fish.
I was elated. My favorite dish!
The meals aboard could not be finer
Than the ones served in the diner.

They had broiled it golden brown and hot.
My elation faded on the spot.
They had served it whole, from head to tail.
That's when my hunger began to fail.

That sweet little fish, fresh from the stream,
Horrified me. I wanted to scream.
That vacant eye stared up at me,
Accusing and dead as it could be.

When I looked, at that lifeless sight,
It took away my appetite.
How could anyone as squeamish as I,
Eat anything that looked me straight in the eye?

Letting the Mind Hang Loose

Sometimes, when I have nothing in particular to think about, I like to let my mind just sort of wander around and see what shows up. It is a nice form of relaxation and conquers stress. That is, provided you don't let it take up subjects like what would happen if you fell into the black hole or flew out into infinity.

Then too, you have to keep some kind of a rein on your mind to keep it from catching onto a refrain from a tune on the radio. That will keep running through your head like a broken record for hours.

I have a mind that is prone to this sort of thing.

One night, just before I was ready to go to sleep, the name Clifford Odets crept in and kept repeating itself over and over. Unlike counting sheep, it did not put me to sleep. I couldn't understand how Mr. Clifford Odets appeared on my mental screen. I had never met the man in my whole life and there he was, like a haunt in my bed. Clifford Odets...Clifford Odets...Clifford Odets, keeping me awake.

I don't recommend any of the above as ways to beat stress. The kind of mind wandering I am suggesting is a more harmless type that deals with the imagination.

The following jingles will give you an idea of what I mean.

Some Thoughts on Gravity

There is a mysterious force called gravity.
Without it life would be a depravity.
Cups and saucers would fly around.
Nothing would hold us to the ground.
At a party it would be a funny feeling,
With everyone wafting around on the ceiling.
It might be fun to float to town,
But how on earth would we ever get down?

I'm not saying we could do without it.
Heavens no! I have no doubt about it.
But I wish that a scientist would...someday,
Work hard in a lab to find a nice way
To lessen the pull just the least little bit,
To release the pressure to which we submit.
Our steps would be lighter.
Our smiles would be brighter.

Imagine the fun of jumping on a bolted down scale,
To find you weigh less than a baby whale.
It would be wonderful to assuage that hunger
For growing old, but looking very much younger.
As we grew older...our cheeks wouldn't sag.
We wouldn't have eyes that tend to bag.
And best of all wouldn't it be yummy,
To never experience a sagging tummy!

Mary Paxton Kirby

Whatever Happened to the Moth?

While cleaning a closet, on my knees, with a cloth,
I wondered—whatever happened—to the moth?
Remember that flutterly, little winged pest,
Who found our wool fabrics so easy to digest?
The moth, seemed to vanish into thin air,
Where did it go then...to find a new lair?

We all know, with the arrival of Orlon and nylon,
There was nothing that this little flier could thrive
on.

Woolen clothing went right out of fashion.
Wash and wear wardrobes became our passion.
So...where, oh, where did the little moth go?
Where, oh, where? I'd be delighted to know.
Since wool was its diet—when we were asleep,
Did it fly outside and inhabit a sheep?
Or is there somewhere a marker for the last known
moth,
Who tried hard to survive by eating synthetic cloth?

Facing Up

There are some unpleasant things in life we have to deal with, whether we like it or not. These realities start even before the first day of school.

There are needles stuck into us for vaccinations, the traumatic trips to the dentists for drilling or braces and the shock of acne in our teens, just to name a few.

We soon learn that these little surprises are nothing compared to the ones we suspect will come later.

The boom starts to lower after we have completed our schooling and are earning a living. Out of nowhere, a man walks into our lives. He shows up almost with our first paycheck.

He is not a shining knight carrying a lance on a white charger. He is toting a briefcase.

He will take you to lunch, woo you with theater tickets and phone you everyday until he finally has you roped and tied. He is an insurance agent.

From this moment on, you find yourself dealing with him and lawyers and others who dim your spirits by acting as constant reminders that in life there is also death. The reality of this is brought home most clearly when you have to make you a will.

Our lawyer, whom we admire and trust, is a very practical man who believes in "telling it like it is."

When I finally got up the nerve to go in and talk to him about this dreary business, he set me straight right away.

I asked a tentative question about a bequest to the children, and he stopped me mid-sentence. I had said, "If I die?"...when he halted my words.

"It is not a question of **if** you die," he said. "You are **going** to die."

For a scary moment or two, I thought it was going to happen immediately, right there in his office.

When the hair on the back of my neck flattened down and I was able to hold a pen in my shaky hand, I signed the document and got the hell out of there.

Later, I discovered that once the visit is over, it is a nice secure feeling to know that you have protected your loved ones.

It is also gratifying to know, too, that by the device of your will you can also create a bit of mischief, to leave behind when you are d—d.

I refuse to look at that last word on paper.

The Importance of a Will

Although it may seem to be depressing
And even just a wee bit distressing,
It's very important that you still
Take the time out to draw up a will
If you have love for your descendants
Or care at all for your dependents.

Otherwise...I want right here to state,
It's wrong for you to die intestate.
So...now before it becomes much too late
Don't let your assets go into probate;
For when you meet the reaper's call...
The courts and taxes will take it all.

Now if your relatives have been unkind
A will can help you pay them back in kind.
I once heard of a lady who...
Gave her relations their just due.
She overheard them say, she'd lost her marbles;
That her mind was gone, her words were garbles.

When they opened her safe to find her will,
They went into shock and are in it still.
They found her will inside of the hopper.
It was all made out and very proper.
She left her money and it was oodles,
To a home and food for indigent poodles.
Her words in the will were certainly not garbles.
She wisely left her heirs...a big bag of marbles!

Children

There is a lot of talk about planned parenthood. You can plan when you *want* to have children and when you can *afford* to have them, but once you get them, there is a lot of guesswork and you find you are in for many surprises.

The parents of a new baby sometimes go into after-birth shock when they bring the baby home from the hospital. Their experienced friends have told them about the colic, 2:00 a.m. feedings and walking a squalling infant in the middle of the night. Undaunted, they go ahead and have the baby anyway.

They soon find out that hearing about these things cannot compare with the actual experience. In the midst of all this chaos, it slowly dawns on the young couple that they will never be alone again. There are three people in the house now, and that third tiny person will demand most of their attention for a very long time.

Later, the parents are made acutely aware of the terrible twos, when their child seems to be all over the place at the same time. Fortunately, this stage passes and in no time, the child is in pre-school, quickly followed by years of elementary and high school, bringing more surprises.

The parents realize that someone is going to have to haul the kid out of bed at an ungodly hour, fix breakfast, pack a lunch and get the child to school on time. This becomes even more difficult if there is no bus. Someone will now become a full time chauffeur for the next sixteen years.

If there is more than one child, there will be countless sleepless nights nursing them through childhood illnesses and colds which are quickly transmitted to the parents.

When the children reach high school, the parents have to deal with the terror filled teens and something called "peer pressure."

It starts with your carefully reared child wanting to be exactly like some young jerk who sets the code of behavior and dress for the whole school enrollment.

Once the parents have survived the teens, and at great expense put them through college, what happens?

They leave home and seldom write unless financially strapped.

Later they marry and move far away from home. Or worse yet, they move in with parents and bring along four grandchildren.

If they have left home for good, the parents sometimes fall victim to the "empty nest syndrome" and buy a dog, or at least a parakeet.

There are times when parents wonder if it was all worth it. If you had the chance, would you do it all over again? You breathe a sigh, look deeply into your heart and you know the answer.

Yes, yes, indeed! You certainly would.

Mary Paxton Kirby

A Look at Having Children

What is this bent for propagation
That brings about this situation?
You bear a child or two or three.
You love them, yes, eternally.

You teach them how to stand on their own,
And find a delight you've never known.
After they have learned to walk,
What a joy, to hear them talk!

It seems that in just no time at all
They're out of your arms and growing tall.
Your life's now focused and directed
To see that they are well protected.

When after the difficult teens are through
You think you will have some time for you.
But you work and save to send them to college
To fill their minds with valued knowledge.

You want them to have the best start in life
To support themselves and perhaps a wife.
In repeating the cycle that you began
You can live your life over, through them, again.
After all the love and tender raising
Fate steps in and it's amazing,
How life can suddenly change your plan.
It's really most hard...to understand.

The careers that you have prepared them for,
Take them away. They're not near any more.
You hear from them, yes...a call or letter
But if you have a choice, a letter is better.
A phone call's so fleeting you forget what to say;
All the things you've been aching to ask them that
   day.
A letter is something to hold and to read
Over and over when you feel the need.

You know that it's right, they cannot stay.
Your nest is empty, they've flown away.
Somehow you never planned it this way.
To be all alone on Christmas Day.

57

Mary Paxton Kirby

Dear Son

Dear Son:

You know how I love to write to you.
I love to write to your brother, too.
Even though we live in an age
When people hardly write a page.

Sometimes I sit and meditate
Until the hour grows very late;
Wondering about the things that you do...
Thinking of things I want to say to you.

I find writing such a compensation.
My very best form of relaxation.
Since you are both so far away
And I can't see you everyday.
It is like a quiet conversation.

When I was young and so very naïve,
No one could tell me, nor could I conceive...
That there would ever come a time
When letter writing would seem so fine.
Of writing in rhyme? I wouldn't believe!

The thing I have learned that makes writing seem
    better,
Is the hope that I too, will soon get a letter,
In answer to the one *I* write, you see.
That is the thought that appeals to me.
A promptly answered, very special letter.

I don't try to write in language grand
But I know that you will understand.
When I get lonely and long for you,
It helps me so, just to write to you.

Though your responses are very few,
I treasure them all and save them, too.
The words in this letter also go for your brother.
They are deep in the heart of...

Your loving,

Mother

Mary Paxton Kirby

Response
(Two months later)

Dear Mother:

Thank you Mother, for your letter.
Glad to know you're feeling better.
I meant to answer weeks ago,
But things get in the way, you know.

I always seem to be on the run,
But last week I had a lot of fun.
It was a weekend, while I was seeing,
A client in Vermont, I went skiing.

In spare time from the office I have to work out.
Today, keeping in shape is what it's all about.
I go to cocktail parties and dinners,
So that I can be among the winners.

From this I'm sure you can surmise,
How much it pays to socialize.
At your request I squeezed time for this letter.
As I said on the phone, I'm glad you're better.

For a while this may be my only one,
As I'm so busy,

Your loving,

Son

P.S. Please try hard not to make a fuss, but,
I can't make it home for Christmas.

The VCR and Other TV Devices

The invention of the video cassette recorder came along at just the right time. Decades ago when television was new and a joy to watch, someone in Washington [Newton Minow, former head of the Federal Communications Commission] called television, "a vast wasteland." I hope he is around to see it now. Network television has, with few exceptions, gone from wasteland to worse.

With the advent of the VCR, at least we can be more selective in our viewing and not be stuck with the shows offered to us by the networks. The device enables us to cull the best offerings, stockpile them, and watch them in prime time in the next evening when the networks are showing sit-coms that have to be sweetened with recorded laughter (to make us think we are watching something funny) or they are running the gamut from sleep inducing to bloody violence.

No invention is perfect and the VCR does have some drawbacks. The fact is, very few of us know how to operate them.

In our house, I am getting a little weary of watching three-quarters of an engrossing movie, then having to write my own ending because we either set the timer wrong or the film in the cassette ran out.

Another very helpful television device is the remote control panel with buttons that enables us to switch channels without leaving the comfort of our chairs. I adore it, especially the mute button.

I actually enjoy a lot of the commercials. However, when they disturb the peace in my house with high decibel soft drink ads, automobile pitchmen screaming their wares or blinding graphics accompanied by the sounds and sight of rockets and bombs coming right at me...I can't tell you how much pleasure I get out of wreaking a little destruction of my own. ZAP!!!

There is one unexpected problem to this ability to change channels from where you sit. It becomes annoying when the zapper is in the hands of a restless husband.

Sneaky TV

The weirdest thing had been happening to me,
Whenever I sat down to look at TV.
I'd be watching "Dallas" and what would I see?
Right in the midst of a torrid love scene,
There would come a close-up of mean Joe Green.

The other night I was watching the news.
The set switched over to "Hill Street Blues"!
I'll admit I was a bit confused.
I had every intent on watching the"Love Boat,"
When up came a picture of a German U-Boat.

I was casing the weather with Willard Scott,
A most affable man, whom we like a lot,
When out the blue, what have I got?
To my surprise and my amazement...
Burt Reynolds burning up the pavement!

After a while, a light dawned bright.
I knew darned well that I was right!
It really made me get uptight.
If this sort of thing is happening to you,
I know the reason. Here's an important clue.

When you take the time to give it a think,
It isn't the TV that's on the blink.
It's just your mate, who, quick as a wink,
Without letting you know of his sneaky intention,
Is changing the channels with a dial-switch
     invention.

Beards

How many more years is it going to take before men go back to being clean-shaven again? I thought beards went out with Abraham Lincoln. Lincoln, bless his heart, had a reason for wearing a beard. His face was terribly pockmarked.

I can understand why the early pioneers wore beards. It kept them from getting frostbitten in the cold winters and they just couldn't pull into a drugstore and pick up a blade on their way west in a covered wagon.

Other than a few reasons like that, it is incomprehensible to me why any man would want to raise a crop of hot, scratchy, unkempt bush on his face. Beards must be murder to wear in the summertime.

I wonder how they keep them clean? After all, a fellow can't just run into the men's room and shampoo his whiskers after every meal, can he?

After watching on television the unkempt, bearded Iranians yelling, "Death to America," why would any man want to choose them to emulate as style-setters?

I have noticed that many men who wear beards have little or no hair on their heads. Is it because they feel that they have to show the world that they can grow hair somewhere?

Come on, guys. Bald can be beautiful. Yul Brenner became a sex symbol displaying a bald head in his role in *The King and I*.

Think about it.

Men Who Wear Beards

When I open my door to a stranger with a beard,
My reaction is panic...someone to be feared.
I'm conditioned to see him raising a fist.
My mind pictures some wild, Mideast terrorist.

I know bearded men are all God's creatures.
But they have few distinguishing features.
Their noses and eyes, I have to memorize
In order that they can be recognized.

I know many nice men who wear beards but...oh
   brother!
I find it so hard to tell one from the other!
Now, I don't mind a neat mustache,
A Van Dyke beard has a lot of panache.

I've sometimes thought it would be rough to be
   kissing,
A man with bristles on a face that was missing.
If a good looking face was under all that hair...
Gee, I'd never be able to know it was there.

I know some women think it's cute
For their sweethearts to be hirsute.
To me, it's a sin and it makes me feel so sad,
For a handsome man to look like a Brillo Pad.

65

Mary Paxton Kirby

The State Lottery

Something puzzles me about the lottery.
Maybe, perchance, I'm getting dottery.
Millions of dollars keep pouring in.
Everyone in the state wants to win.

With hundreds of thousands of number choosers,
Ninety-nine percent are always the losers.
We know our chances are small to win,
But it's fun to participate in.

Before we went out and voted it in,
The politicians were promising then,
That it would provide better roads and schools.
We fell for their pitch, but were we all fools?

They promised great things and even lower taxes,
But after all this time, we find that the fact is,
Nothing much has changed, and I'd like to inquire,
"Why is it that our taxes keep going higher?"

Reading About the Rich and Famous

Living a comparatively quiet life out of the mainstream, I would like to catch up now and then about what's going on in the world of the jet setters. It takes my mind off of things such as: Are we heading for another depression? Will the stock market crash again? Will Ted Kennedy really try again for the presidency? Things like that.

Reading about the latest antics of the movie stars and the misbehavior of some of our elected officials and clergy is escapism in its purest form.

Now you can find this in most any newspaper, but it's not much fun. When they have a juicy story, they are inclined to attribute the tale to "a reliable source" and keep me trying to guess who squealed. I am not inclined to believe words of a source who refuses to give his name.

Indeed, if you want the facts about the private lives of the rich and famous, the only place to go is to the tabloids.

They have been sued so many times that they have to be damn careful. If they print the name...they have got the goods on the guy.

Mary Paxton Kirby

The National Enquirer

Tell me if you think it's wrong to admit,
That every week I go out and buy it?
Most every issue I am an acquirer,
Of a paper called *The National Enquirer*

Friends and family are prone to gag,
And ask me why I buy that "rag."
It's "in" for people to turn up a nose,
When I come home with one of those.

In the evening when I am busy cooking,
And they are sure there is no one looking,
Just out of the corner of my eye,
I catch a glimpse of some sneaky guy,
Taking it with him down the hall;
The Enquirer, lurid headlines and all.

If you don't take it seriously,
There's really no crime that I can see.
It's like a printed version of an old sideshow,
Under a circus tent, where we all used to go.
It's filled with barkers, freaks and medicine men.
Why is it *déclassé*, to read now and then?
It only comes out once a week, and not daily.
They've just stolen a page from Barnum and Bailey.

Holidays

In my opinion, there are too many holidays. Maybe that is because my husband and I are retired. To retirees, a holiday means the banks are closed and there is no mail delivery. Going to the mailbox is an important part of our daily routine. Holidays are great for people who go to work, and, children would band together and rebel if someone tried to take away even one of their legal school holidays.

It seems to me that we hardly get through with one holiday before another one turns up. It has gotten all out of hand. My husband is convinced that Mother's and Father's days, and now Mother-in-law and Grandparents' days were dreamed up by some schemer at a greeting card company to make us spend more money.

Friends of ours had a beautiful home on an island in the West Indies. They lived there for many years. During that time, the government declared so many holidays that the post office could not keep up with the mail and it mounted up. The post office workers solved the problem. When so much back mail began to get unwieldy, they threw it in a corner of the room and started over with the next batch that arrived. Dependent on the mail for their livelihood, our friends had to sell their house and move back to the States.

Have you noticed how slowly the mail arrives after a holiday here in the U.S. lately? Could we be heading for the same problem?

What I really started out to write about was the way some people react to certain holidays.

The following jingle explains my way of telling my husband not to be a holiday Scrooge.

Mary Paxton Kirby

Holidays
(Like Mother's Day and Father's)

Dearest:

You told me you thought Mother's
　and Father's Days,
Were just gimmicks dreamed up by
　merchants for ways
To drum up trade; keep us running to stores,
To keep us hopping with even more chores.

You don't let them get to **you!** Do you, honey?
They're not going to bilk you out of your money!
It's a ruse you consider monumental
To play on the hearts of the sentimental!

Sooo...even though it was very hard,
I didn't buy you a present or card.
Back in my office I hunted around.
An old piece of paper I finally found.

It didn't cost me a single cent.
My dear, you see I am really bent,
On giving you something, on your day,
To say I love you anyway!

Your loving wife,

Happy Father's Day!!!

Mary Paxton Kirby

What's His Name?

There was a young man from the Middle East,
Who had no direction, not in the least.
He wanted to attain some claim to fame,
So people would remember his face, his name.
He was going to have his day in the sun,
If he had to get it with a gun.

Without fame he felt he couldn't exist.
He decided to become a terrorist.
He thought if he were part of a terrible plot,
Television cameras would make him a big shot.
He'd get his picture on the screen,
Waving his fists and looking mean.

He saw to it that he was well-armed.
Cared not a hoot about who he harmed.
He loaded explosives into a van
And into an embassy wall he ran.
The blast was heard for many miles around,
Creating havoc all over the town.

It blew him straight to kingdom come.
All because he wanted some
Recognition, some fleeting fame,
So somebody would remember his name.
There was nothing left of him when he took his fall.
So nobody took a picture of him at all.

The only thing about him that people remembered,
Was that he was some fiend whose body was
   dismembered.

72

A Special Tribute

At this time, I would like to forget about things that are annoying and write about one of the many good things that has happened in my life. It was the day that Nolia Hunter walked to our front door. She is one of those special people whom you love and will remember for the rest of your life. I don't know what I would ever do without her!

To Nolia, With Love

It was a lucky day when Nolia came into my life,
To relieve the burdens of a harried housewife.
I expected to see someone dressed in
    work clothes.
Not Nolia! No, Nolia would never stoop to those.

She came dancing in with brushes and pail,
Dressed up and clean to the last fingernail.
Her bright smile was enough to dim the sun.
Her laughter brought joy to us, everyone.

Her sense of humor, so bright and gay
Can make us laugh on the darkest day.
She attacks the house like it is her own.
She sings at her work in a mellow tone.

At first I thought she was talking to herself,
While she was up on a ladder cleaning a shelf.
But no, it was God, she was speaking to.
I learned that to her this was nothing new.

She took God with her wherever she went.
She spreads His love until her day is spent.
Though she has had troubles, far more
    than her share,
She has met them bravely, with faith left to spare.

No matter what the world has given her to face,
Her smile never wavers, she takes troubles
    with grace.
She spends her life in the service of others.
Loves them as though they were sisters
    and brothers.

This little poem doesn't begin to touch,
The things about her I want to say so much.
I could go on and on and never end
About Nolia, who's become my most loved friend.

Poems of Inspiration—
From the Heart

Remembering

Today I climbed a far off hill
Where I had been with you;
Nature had blended with deftness and skill
Sky and earth in a hazy blue.

The heavens were still and undisturbed
Save for the movement of a downy white cloud.
The leaves on the trees were unperturbed
Concealing their branches in a cool green shroud.

The sun shone down on the housetops below
That seemed so tiny from my lofty perch;
So varied in color they formed a warm glow,
Like stained glass windows on an old, old church.

As I gazed upon this vast panorama,
There suddenly seemed to fall,
With just a touch of melodrama,
An empty sickening pall.

For I realized beauty, from this high plane,
Held not the loveliness I used to view.
Although I was sure the scene was the same,
The thing that was lacking, I know, was you.

God's Gift, the Sunrise

What is more glorious than the sight of the sun
    rising in the morning.
Heralding the new day, dawning low on the
    horizon.
Lighting the world and all its wonders
Delighting our eyes, our minds, our souls.
More beautiful even than the flamboyant sunsets
That denote days ending. The sunrise promises
    a new beginning.
Darkness disappears, hope comes, and with it
The will to begin our lives anew; to nurture the
Spark within that makes us one with God.
Oh, the comfort of knowing that as this world
    takes a spin,
Tomorrow the celestial light will come again.
Although, at times, its golden rays may be
    covered
By shrouds of dark gray clouds that hide it
From our sight, in our hearts we know it's there.
Oh, sunrise...radiant sunrise....
God's gift and message for all to behold,
That like the sun, God, too, is there.
'Though we can't see Him through our limited
    vision
We can feel His warmth, His never ending love
And His protective care.

My Dawn Comes Softly

What could that poet have been thinking of
When he looked at the changing sky above?
What inspired him to write a song that day
As he waited for dawn in Mandalay?
What kind of spell was that bard under,
When he wrote that sun comes up like thunder?
Not ever have I beheld such a sight,
When I greet the morn at the end of the night.
To me, dawn appears as a soft pink light,
Arising gently from the shroud of night.
A lady awakening from her sleep,
To spread her beauty out over the deep
Darkness of the sea...to touch it with blue,
And light up the sky with its pastel hue.
My dawn's not one that breaks clouds asunder,
And smashes into day with a clap of thunder.
My dawn is one that softly comes and goes,
Making her appearance on rosy toes,
Before the sun rises on its bright way
And sweeps the wispy skirts of dawn away.

I Looked to the Hills

Early one morning when I arose from my bed,
I sat by my window. As my Bible had said,
I looked over the still lake and up to the hills.
I was hoping to find ease from all of my ills.
I prayed that up there my God I would find,
To heal my spirit, my body, my mind.

When He wasn't there, I closed my eyes.
Gone were the hills...all my earthly ties
To the land, the birds, the flowers, the trees;
All of the world that one usually sees.
In that velvety darkness, I looked deep inside
And found Him...where the quiet and the soul
    abide.

Soft Music

Some music is so sweet–soul filling,
Spine tingling, head filling...thrilling.
I snuggle into it and let it wrap me
In its folds of lovely sound.
I nestle in it, content to abide there
In this musical womb....
Like eiderdown.
Soft as lying on a cloud
Gently swelling...never loud.
Such a lovely limbo where I am alone.
Age and ills
Are stilled,
And I am one with tone.

With Love to Tyler Paxton Kirby — From his Grandmother, Pax

It is said that when a child such as this one is born, he doesn't come alone. At the time that this little boy was due to come into the world, the sky was a deep, dark blue, sprinkled with twinkling stars. People craned their necks to see the light that night.

One star suddenly broke away from all the others and streaked across the heavens. The star was on its sole mission to bring this baby safely down to earth, on the October night of his birth.

The star that had been content to lie quietly for hundreds of years, shining its light in the dark blue of the night, suddenly blinked nervously, and seemed to rock from side to side because it knew the time had come to carry out the mission for which it was created. On his trip to the world, the baby was touched by the finger of an angel who gave him a smile that would melt an iron.

This baby was given the gift of love and warmth. Once, in a shoe store, he walked up to a stranger— a lady with sadness in her eyes. Although he didn't know her, the little toddler moved over close to her, put his arms around her neck and gave her a kiss which took away the sadness, and her lips turned to a smile.

May his life be long, his dreams fulfilled, and all his days be happy, healthy and strong.

Love Before First Sight

Repeated by request from *While Morning Stars Sang*,
(for Spencer Cooper Kirby, before his birth)

I have never seen him.
I don't know if his eyes
Are green or blue.
I only know...I love him.

He will come to me from
Some far off cosmic place,
Away beyond my ken,
Known only to God, not men.

There are certain things
I am sure about him
That make me know it will be love...
Even before first sight.

It is written
That we shall love.
It is in his stars.
It is my destiny.

He will arrive in the light
Of the bright August moon.
I await his coming
With arms open wide.

Oh, how long I have waited
For this son of my son.
God, please heap blessings
On my precious grandson.

God Bless This Child

(Written for Alexander Daniel Kirby before his birth)
Reprinted by request, from *While Morning Stars Sang*

A new little life is on its way.
May it greet the world on a sunny day.
May the skies be blue as the baby's eyes,
On the day it sees its first sunrise.

God grant that this baby be perfect and strong.
Give this child a happy life and one that's long.
Bless it with a lively mind.
Make it gentle, loving, kind.

Let it live in a world of peace on earth,
From the very first day of this child's birth.
May it inherit all good from its Mother and
    Daddy.
May it face life bravely and seldom be sad.

God, please bless it with beautiful features
And abiding love for all Your creatures.
Let this child bring its parents bountiful joy,
Be it a little girl or a baby boy,
God bless this child.

Patience

Don't be afraid to start again.
Have patience with life's strife and pain.

Make each day a bright new start.
Just keep knowing in your heart.

It takes trial and error to perfect,
To reach the goal that you expect.

God didn't make the world in a minute,
Not with all His power infinite.

Patience is the thing that pays.
It even took HIM seven days!

You Can Do It!

If you have a dream,
Pursue it.
An inspiration?
Woo it.
'Tis the hand of God
Tapping at your heart
To tell you—
You can do it!

Mary Paxton Kirby

She Loves Me

Her love for me is beyond conception.
Unparalleled without exception.
She gives me all of her attention.
Her lapses are too slight to mention.
She's single-minded in her devotion.
Her eyes shine bright with deep emotion.
She loves me when I'm wide awake,
And when I sleep, she's there to take
Care of me from every harm.
In bed, she snuggles, keeps me warm.
She loves me truly, like no other,
Sister, brother, kids or mother.
Oh, it's so very plain to see,
She gives her love to only me.
Other people may come around,
But when they do, she turns them down.
She gaily greets them, but lets me know
She's mine again when at last they go.
Who is capable of so much love?
Was sent to me from heav'n above?
Who means the world and all to me?
My tiny poodle. Her name? Bonnie.

The Invisible Tie

Love is an invisible tie that binds
Us with a silver string that winds
As far away as you may go, into space or sea,
And gently, oh so gently, draws you back to me.

It wraps us close when we are together.
Keeps us faithful through stormy weather.
As long as we love we will never be,
Separate here, or in eternity.

Friendship

Friendship
Is better than kinship.
Why do you suppose it?
It's because we chose it!

Love is Forever

(written for my son, Dennis, and his fiancee,
Barbara Moscow, for their wedding, May 18, 1985)

Love is giving

Love is forgiving.

Love cares.

Love shares.

Love understands,

Never demands.

Love does not smother,

Trusts one another.

Love holds us together.

Love is forever.

The Chickadee

This has been my observation,
Watching at a feeding station.
The Chickadee, a tiny mite,
Is swift and darting in his flight.
He comes to the feeder and waits his turn,
From greedy birds who never learn,
To make a little bit of space,
For someone else to take a place.
They fight and push and crowd and shove,
Without a shred of selfless love.

The Chickadee sits and waits so sweetly,
For them to gorge themselves completely,
Somewhere inside it is innate,
For him to bide his time and wait.
When it is his turn to fill his need,
The little darling takes just one seed.
He flies away with it to a tree.
A lesson perhaps for you and me?
A Chickadee knows it's only right,
For everybody to be polite.

About the Author

The prose, verse and art included in this book represent a major portion of Pax Kirby's *Jingles for the Jangled*. Other witty and insightful selections were included in the 1991 Tabby House anthology, *While Morning Stars Sang*. Her delightful "jingles" and essays are commentary on life from the perspective of a successful writer, radio and television director at a Park Avenue advertising agency, and singer. She is the beloved wife of radio and television star, Durward Kirby, whose autobiography, *My Life...Those Wonderful Years!* was recently published. The Kirbys have two sons, Dennis and Randy, and three grandsons. Her many talents also include painting.

In 1983, Pax published her successful and charming book, *The View from Under the Table,* an authoritative look at the Kirby household by their poodle, Bonnie. Illustrations for her books were provided by their friend, internationally-known illustrator, Mel Crawford.

The Kirbys spend their winters in Florida and their summers in Connecticut.